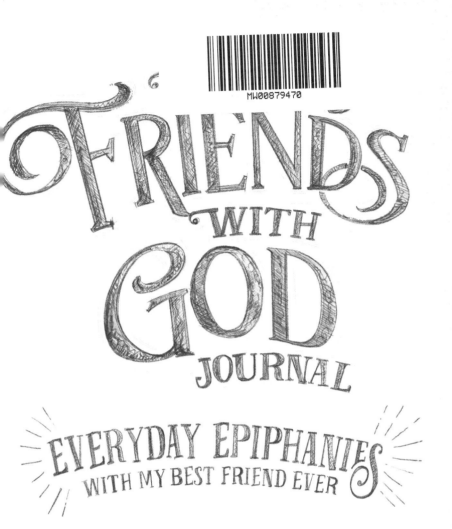

FRIENDS WITH GOD JOURNAL

EVERYDAY EPIPHANIES
WITH MY BEST FRIEND EVER

WRITTEN BY JEFF WHITE

ILLUSTRATED BY DAVID HARRINGTON

THIS JOURNAL IS ALL ABOUT

_____
(my name)

and my best friend,

GOD!

_____
Date

Visit MyLifetree.com/Kids for more fun, faith-building stuff for kids!

I Am Friends With God Journal
Everyday Epiphanies With My Best Friend Ever

Copyright © 2018 Group Publishing, Inc./0000 0001 0362 4853
Lifetree™ is an imprint of Group Publishing, Inc.

group.com

Written by Jeff White
Illustrated by David Harrington
Chief Creative Officer: Joani Schultz
Senior Editor: Candace McMahan
Designer: Darrin Stoll
Assistant Editor: Cherie Shifflett

ISBN: 978-1-4707-5315-3 (softcover)

Printed in the United States of America.
001 USA 0718
10 9 8 7 6 5 4 3 2 1   27 26 25 24 23 22 21 20 19 18

Hi, Friend!

Did you know you can see God all around you? It's true! God is a part of your life every day and is *always* busy. You may not be able to see God, but you *can* see what God is doing...if you know where to look.

This fun faith journal gives you the chance to explore God's wonderful world while sharing *tons* of things about *you*. It's exciting to discover how God is connected to *every* part of your life. And it even shows you where to find more about me in the Bible.

What's an epiphany (ee-PIFF-an-ee)? It's seeing that God is real in your life. Sometimes God surprises you, sometimes God makes you smile, and sometimes God makes you go, "Wow!" This journal will show you how to see and hear God in real ways.

So have fun! Be creative! And be who God created you to be!

Your ever-loving friend,

Jesus

"So now we can rejoice in our wonderful new relationship with God because our Lord Jesus Christ has made us friends of God."

(Romans 5:11)

YOU ARE GOD'S FRIEND

And this faith journal is like the *Friends With God Story Bible's* friend. They go hand in hand. You can read the story Bible to explore how Bible characters had a real friendship with God.

And this faith journal helps you explore *your* friendship with God.

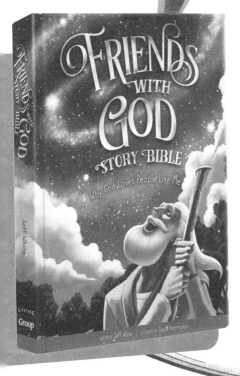

Read the *Friends With God Story Bible!*

Just as he is a friend to the characters in the *Friends With God Story Bible,* God is your friend in every part of your life.

- God helped young David fight a giant. What battles will God help you win?

- God helped Esther be brave. How is God helping you be brave?

- God kept Daniel safe from the lions. When does God keep you safe?

Read the story Bible; then write and draw about *your* life in this journal. The more you discover about God, the more you'll discover about yourself.

Take a PIP Quiz!

What's a PIP Quiz? PIP is short for "ePIPhany"— seeing God in your life. Whenever you see a PIP Quiz in this journal, answer in your own way to share how you've seen God at work around you.

GOD Doesn't Make Mistakes

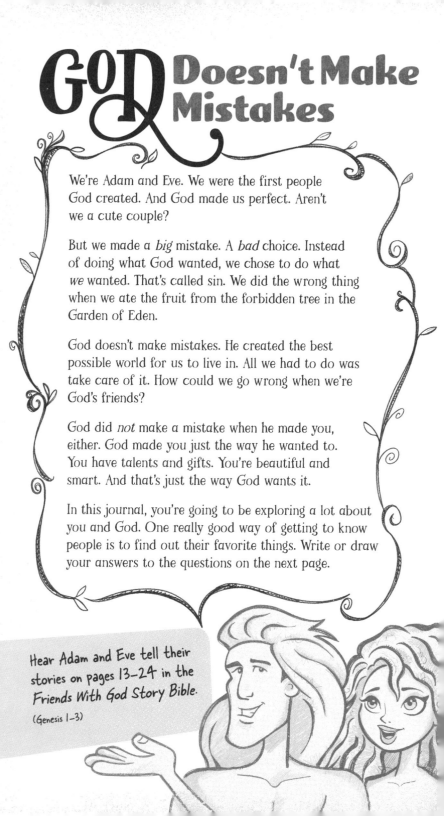

We're Adam and Eve. We were the first people God created. And God made us perfect. Aren't we a cute couple?

But we made a *big* mistake. A *bad* choice. Instead of doing what God wanted, we chose to do what *we* wanted. That's called sin. We did the wrong thing when we ate the fruit from the forbidden tree in the Garden of Eden.

God doesn't make mistakes. He created the best possible world for us to live in. All we had to do was take care of it. How could we go wrong when we're God's friends?

God did *not* make a mistake when he made you, either. God made you just the way he wanted to. You have talents and gifts. You're beautiful and smart. And that's just the way God wants it.

In this journal, you're going to be exploring a lot about you and God. One really good way of getting to know people is to find out their favorite things. Write or draw your answers to the questions on the next page.

Hear Adam and Eve tell their stories on pages 13–24 in the *Friends With God Story Bible*.

(Genesis 1–3)

What's your favorite thing God made about you?

What's one mistake you've made?

What's one thing you learned from your mistake?

Three Epic Epiphanies

1. God is your perfect friend and doesn't make mistakes.

2. God loves you just the way he made you.

3. "For we are God's masterpiece. He has created us anew in Christ Jesus, so we can do the good things he planned for us long ago" (Ephesians 2:10).

Favorite Things

"Whatever is good and perfect is a gift coming down to us from God our Father." (James 1:17)

God gave us a lot of good things in the Garden of Eden. The Bible says that the things we enjoy in life are gifts from God. Your favorite things are signs that God is with you and loves you. Write some of your favorite things below.

About Me...

Favorite hobby:

Favorite thing to draw:

Favorite song to sing:

Favorite thing about me that's different:

Favorite thing to paint on my face:

Favorite thing about me that nobody knows:

Favorite way to goof off:

Favorite talent:

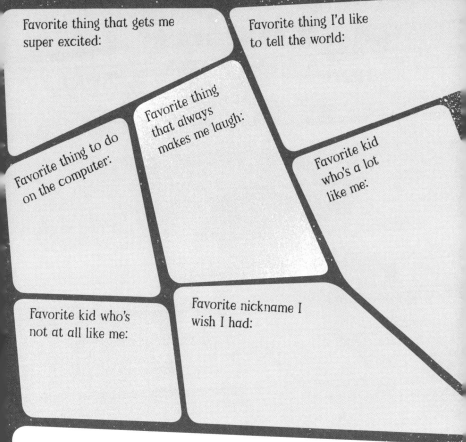

Favorite thing that gets me super excited:

Favorite thing I'd like to tell the world:

Favorite thing that always makes me laugh:

Favorite thing to do on the computer:

Favorite kid who's a lot like me:

Favorite kid who's not at all like me:

Favorite nickname I wish I had:

About God...

What do you think is God's favorite thing about you that's different?

What do you think is God's favorite nickname?

Here are some examples from the Bible:

I Am
Exodus 3:14

Alpha and Omega
(Beginning and End)
Revelation 22:13

Good
Psalm 119:68

King of Kings
1 Timothy 6:15

Omnipotent
(All-Powerful)
Jeremiah 32:17-18

Love
1 John 4:7-10

The Provider
Genesis 22:9-14

Peace
Judges 6:16-24

Creator
Genesis 1:1

The Holy One
Revelation 4:8-11

The Healer
Exodus 15:22-26

The Giver
Acts 17:24-28

Comforter
2 Corinthians 1:3-4

Almighty
Genesis 49:25

Father
Romans 8:15-17

Friend
Romans 5:11

My Life in P.I.E.
(Personal Identity Enhancement)

How Adam and Eve Might
Have Spent Their Day in
the Garden of Eden

10% Sleeping in Grass
30% Naming Animals
5% Eating Fruit
45% Talking to God
10% Frolicking

"Wherever your treasure is,
there the desires of your
heart will also be." (Luke 12:34)

 QUIZ! How is spending time with God like
spending time with your friends?

Fill out these P.I.E. charts to show what makes you, you.

How I Like to Spend Time With God

Chart the things you do and how often you do them.

- [ ] Talk to God
- [ ] Read my Bible
- [ ] Read books about God
- [ ] Listen to music about God
- [ ] Use my talents
- [ ] Worship God
- [ ] Make art
- [ ] Be outside in nature
- [ ] Something else:

How I Spend Time With My Friends

Chart the things you do and how often you do them.

- [ ] Play games
- [ ] Talk
- [ ] Listen to music
- [ ] Hang out
- [ ] Play on a team together
- [ ] Eat
- [ ] Watch videos
- [ ] Something else:

Making the Most of It

God is the master of "mosts"—the most powerful, the most loving, the most forgiving, and the most awesome friend anyone could ever have. When God created the world, he made it the most wonderful place for us to live. And when God created you, he gave you a *ton* of "mosts." List some of yours below.

The person I'd most like to get to know better:

The person I admire the most:

The class in school I like most:

The most generous thing I'd like to do:

The hardest thing I've ever done:

The thing that's easiest for me to do:

The most adventurous thing I've ever done:

The thing about me that's most different from anyone else:

The happiest I've ever felt:

The most trouble I've ever been in:

The person I'm most thankful for:

My Top Fives

Top Five Things God Created

Top Five Gifts I've Been Given

PIP QUIZ!

One of the ways God loves us is through other people (see 2 Corinthians 5:20). Who in your life shows God's love to you the most?

My favorite book

My Bookshelf

Books are awesome. What books are on your bookshelf? What are your favorite books? What books do you hope to read someday?

Write the titles of your favorite books on these shelves. On this page, draw the cover of your very favorite book. On the bottom shelf on the next page, draw a new cover for the best book ever, the Holy Bible.

"People do not live by bread alone, but by every word that comes from the mouth of God."

(Matthew 4:4)

YES? NO? MAYBE?

Just like Adam and Eve, God made you unique. No one else who ever lived is exactly like you. You have different interests, talents, and goals. Here's your chance to decide which kinds of things you'd do...or not.

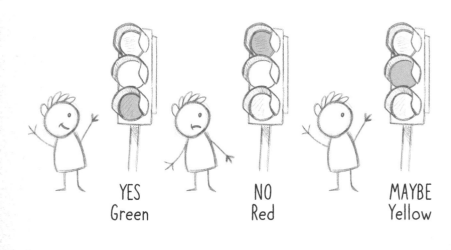

YES
Green

NO
Red

MAYBE
Yellow

Color in the lights to show what you think about the stuff below.

Do you want to...

- sing in a rock band?
- write a book?
- drive a bulldozer?
- train a dog?
- play quarterback?
- fly an airplane?
- perform surgery?

Would you...

- want to know how long you'll live?
- like to stay a kid the rest of your life?
- want to be an adult right now?
- trade lives with a celebrity?
- like to bring your favorite fictional character to life?
- want to read your best friend's mind?
- live in a zoo for a year?

Would you like to...

- travel through time?
- travel to Mars?
- travel to the bottom of the ocean?
- travel by camel through the desert?
- travel to the moon?
- travel by horse across America?
- travel barefoot the rest of your life?

Would you wear this costume?

- princess
- ninja
- cowboy or cowgirl
- clown
- villain
- soldier
- robot

Talk to God

God loves it when we talk with him—just as best friends do. Praying is easy. All you have to do is tell God what you're thinking. You can ask God questions, tell him what you're worried about, or thank him for the things he's given you.

Here are some ideas for what you can pray about:

- Thank God for what you've learned in the Bible.

- Ask God to help you make the right choices.

- Tell God about one way you know he's real.

Write down what you prayed right here:

STOP
— AND —
GO

Stop what you're doing and go do something for God! Write down the names of three friends or family members here. Next to each name, write one thing that's unique or special about that person. Then tell each person—today—what you love about each one that's so unique. Call them, text them, write them a note—whatever you like best.

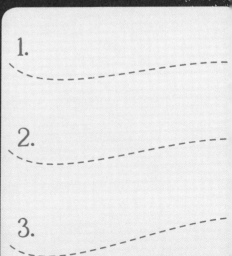

1.

2.

3.

GOD Sticks With YOU

My name is Noah. I like to think I'm a good guy. There was a time when I was the *only* good guy in a world full of bad guys. So I was very glad when God said he would save me and my family from a *giant flood* that would destroy everything in the world.

I got a second chance because I was God's friend. I love God and do things that make God happy. And God has stuck with me, just like a true friend.

You are God's friend, too. And, like a loyal, loving friend, God will always stick with you. He does that because of his grace, which is a word that means being given something good even though you don't deserve it.

God loves you and helps you, even when you mess up. God is the kind of friend who lets you try again when you fail. God never gives up on you!

Hear Noah tell his story on page 25 in the Friends With God Story Bible.
(Genesis 6:9–9:17)

How do you feel when you get a second chance to do the right thing?

When have you given someone a second chance?

Draw how your face looks
when someone gives you
a second chance.

Three Epic Epiphanies

1. God loves you.

2. Even better than a human friend, God promises to always be
   with you.

3. "Do not be afraid or discouraged, for the Lord will personally
   go ahead of you. He will be with you; he will neither fail you
   nor abandon you" (Deuteronomy 31:8).

Like a
RAINBOW

Draw three things you've seen in your life that remind you of God.

What Makes a HERO?

I'm Noah. People call me a hero because I loved God and saved the animals. There are lots of other kinds of heroes, too. Some real heroes are in the Bible, and some real heroes, such as firefighters and nurses, are alive today. Other heroes are pretend, but they help us know what a hero should be like. Whenever you have courage or help someone, you can be a hero, too.

"Through their faith, the people in days of old earned a good reputation." (Hebrews 11:2)

Which Bible hero is your favorite?

- ☐ Young David vs. Goliath *(1 Samuel 17)*
- ☐ Queen Esther vs. Haman *(Esther 5-8)*
- ☐ Daniel vs. the lions *(Daniel 6)*
- ☐ Moses vs. Pharaoh *(Exodus 7-12)*
- ☐ Gideon vs. the Midianites *(Judges 6-7)*
- ☐ Joshua vs. Jericho *(Joshua 6)*
- ☐ Someone else:

Which comic book hero is your favorite?

- ☐ Superman
- ☐ Batman
- ☐ Spider-Man
- ☐ Thor
- ☐ Iron Man
- ☐ Wonder Woman
- ☐ Wolverine
- ☐ Black Panther
- ☐ Captain America
- ☐ Someone else:

Draw a picture of your favorite Bible and comic book heroes here, and write their greatest strength in one word.

Mightiest Bible Hero

GREATEST STRENGTH

Mightiest Comic Book Hero

GREATEST STRENGTH

PIP QUIZ!

What's one way you could be a hero for God?

My Life in P.I.E.
(Personal Identity Enhancement)

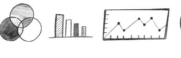

"You must honor God with your body." (1 Corinthians 6:20)

5%

10%

45%

30%

How Noah Might Have Spent His Day on the Ark

45% Feeding the animals

30% Sleeping

10% Checking for leaks

5% Eating

 QUIZ!

Describe what you think it means to be "thirsty" for God.

Things I Like to Do With Water

Draw the activities you like—and how much you like them—in your P.I.E. chart:

Drink it

Swim in it

Take a bath in it

Shower in it

Ski on it

Sail on it

Fish in it

Jump into it

Something else:

My Favorite Bible Stories About Water

Rank how much you like each of these Bible stories:

1

2

3

4

5

6

7

8

Noah and the flood *(Genesis 6-9)*

Moses parting the Red Sea *(Exodus 14)*

Jonah and the big fish *(Jonah 1-4)*

John the Baptist baptizing Jesus *(John 1:19-34)*

Jesus turning water into wine *(John 2:1-11)*

Peter walking on the water *(Matthew 14:22-33)*

Jesus washing his disciples' feet *(John 13:1-17)*

Something else:

I had a *lot* of animals on my ark. It was kind of like having an entire zoo full of pets! What do you think makes a good pet?

The Perfect PET

PIP QUIZ!

What's one thing you can learn about God from all the animals he created?

Fill in the chart below to show which animals you think would make good or not-so-good pets.

	Worst pet ever!	Kinda boring.	Probably not awesome.	I guess it's okay.	Sounds like a good one.	Love, love, love!
Mouse						
Dog						
Cat						
Goldfish						
Hermit Crab						
Goat						
Horse						
Pig						
Lizard						
Snake						
Chicken						
Guinea Pig						
Duck						
Canary						
Parrot						
Llama						
Ferret						
Rabbit						
Hedgehog						
Gerbil						
Cockatoo						
Frog						
Turtle						
Tarantula						

My ZOO

One of the ways God shows he cares about you is by giving you responsibilities—a big word that means "important things to do." God knows what you can do best, so whenever he asks you to do something, he knows you can do it.

If God wanted you to take care of a bunch of animals, which ones would you like to take care of? Fill in this map of a zoo by drawing pictures or writing the names of the animals you like best.

"To those who use well what they are given, even more will be given, and they will have an abundance."
(Matthew 25:29)

GOD'S Amazing Animals

"Just ask the animals, and they will teach you. Ask the birds of the sky, and they will tell you. Speak to the earth, and it will instruct you. Let the fish in the sea speak to you." (Job 12:7-8)

About Me...

Favorite mammal: ....

Favorite bird: ....

Favorite sea creature: ....

Favorite reptile: ....

Favorite farm animal: ....

Favorite forest animal: ....

Favorite small animal: ....

Favorite large animal: ....

Animal I feel like most of the time: ....

Favorite animal sound: ....

Favorite animal to wear on a T-shirt: ....

About God...

Sometimes the Bible uses animals as symbols for different aspects of God's character. Which of these describes God best as your friend?

☐ **Lamb** (John 1:29)

☐ **Lion** (Revelation 5:5-6; Hosea 11:10)

☐ **Mother Hen** (Matthew 23:37)

☐ **Worm** (Psalm 22:6)

☐ **Bronze Serpent** (John 3:14-15)

☐ **Ox** (Numbers 24:8)

☐ **Dove** (Matthew 3:16)

 **QUIZ!**

How does nature show you that God is real?
(Read about it in Romans 1:19-20 and Psalm 8:3-4.)

The Promise KEEPER

My name is Abraham. People called me a friend of God. That's because I trusted God with everything in my life, even when it didn't make sense to me. I always knew God wanted the best for me and my family, so I believed him—no matter what.

God is such a faithful friend that he made me some amazing promises. He promised me a big family, and then he gave me a *huge* family—more than all the stars you can count in the sky.

Like a perfect friend, God keeps his promises. And God has promised you a lot of things, too. He promises to take care of all your needs, and he promises to never leave your side. God is always there for you.

Hear Abraham tell his story on page 31 in the *Friends With God Story Bible*. (Genesis 15)

How does it make you feel to know that God keeps his promises to you?

When have you made a promise to someone? What happened?

Draw how your face
looks when someone
keeps a promise to you.

Three Epic Epiphanies

1. God keeps his promises.

2. God promises to always be your friend.

3. "For all of God's promises have been fulfilled in Christ
   with a resounding 'Yes!' " (2 Corinthians 1:20).

My Life in P.I.E.
(Personal Identity Enhancement)

Things I Pray For

Chart how much you pray for the following things.

- Things I need
- Things I want
- My family
- My friends
- Giving thanks
- God's help
- Things I don't understand
- Something else:

My Day

Chart how much time you spend doing each activity. Each slice = 1 hour.

- Playing outside
- Sleeping
- Eating
- Reading
- Watching a screen
- Playing a game
- Talking
- Going to school
- Being awesome
- Something else:

Kinds of Pie I Like

Chart your favorite kinds of pie.

- ☐ Cherry
- ☐ Apple
- ☐ Pumpkin
- ☐ Chocolate cream
- ☐ Pecan
- ☐ Banana cream
- ☐ Key lime
- ☐ Lemon
- ☐ Other:

PIP QUIZ!

What do you think God spends his time doing every day?
(If you're not sure, find a clue in Proverbs 15:3.)

What I Like to EAT

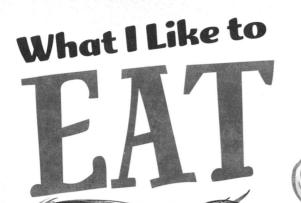

Hello. I'm Jacob. Back in my day, food brought friends together. We ate roasted meat, bread, nuts, yogurt, honey, milk—it was all delicious! I was a great cook, too. Usually I used my cooking skills for good, but sometimes I used them for selfish reasons, too. (You can read more about it in Genesis 27.)

"Go ahead! Eat your food with joy...God approves!" (Ecclesiastes 9:7)

PIP QUIZ!

How can food be a reminder of your friendship with God? (If you're not sure, find a clue in 1 Corinthians 10:31.)

List your three favorite...

Vegetables:

Fruits:

Meats:

Cereals:

Flavors of ice cream:

Pizza toppings:

Crunchy foods:

Chewy foods:

Red foods:

Green foods:

Yellow foods:

Foods to dip in ketchup:

Wonderfully MADE

The most wonderful things about what God provides for me.

Food

The most delicious thing I've ever eaten:

The biggest thing I've ever eaten:

The grossest thing I've ever tasted:

The hottest thing I've ever tasted:

The spiciest food I've ever eaten:

The slimiest food I've ever eaten:

The saltiest food I've ever eaten:

The stickiest food I've ever eaten:

The best-smelling food:

The food I could eat the most of:

The worst-smelling food:

The best restaurant I've ever eaten in:

The food I'll never, ever eat again:

 QUIZ!

What does it say about your best friend, God, that he'd give you so many delicious things to eat? (If you're not sure, find a clue in Matthew 6:25-34.)

Talk to GOD

God is your forever friend, so you can talk to him about anything. God wants to hear whatever you have to say. You can tell him about your day, you can tell him what you're afraid of, and you can even tell him a funny joke!

Take a minute or two to pray right now, and write down what you prayed about here:

Thank God for a promise he's made to you.

Tell God how much you love him.

Talk with God about what's on your mind.

STOP —AND— GO

Stop what you're doing and *go* do something for God! Like friends, God loves it when we're generous. Right now, donate something of yours to charity. Find five pieces of clothing, five toys, five books, five cans of food—five of anything— and put them in a box. Ask a grown-up in your life to donate them to a charity that can give them to someone who needs them.

List the five things you gave away here:

1.

2.

3.

4.

5.

♡ Love It!
👍 Like It.
🚫 Loathe It...

My name is Miriam. When the people of Israel and I were living in the wilderness, there wasn't much to eat. But God was always watching out for us. God gave us a food called manna, which tasted like cake made from honey. We called it bread from heaven. Every morning we'd go out and collect it off the ground, and every day we'd have plenty to keep our stomachs full.

What food can't you get enough of? What food is just okay? What food do you never want to see again? Circle your answers below.

Veggies

♡ 👍 🚫 Onions
♡ 👍 🚫 Peas
♡ 👍 🚫 Green Beans
♡ 👍 🚫 Spinach
♡ 👍 🚫 Carrots
♡ 👍 🚫 Celery
♡ 👍 🚫 Broccoli
♡ 👍 🚫 Cucumbers

Proteins

♡ 👍 🚫 Chicken
♡ 👍 🚫 Beef
♡ 👍 🚫 Lamb
♡ 👍 🚫 Fish
♡ 👍 🚫 Bacon
♡ 👍 🚫 Eggs
♡ 👍 🚫 Shrimp

Fruits

♡ 👍 🚫 Apples
♡ 👍 🚫 Oranges
♡ 👍 🚫 Bananas
♡ 👍 🚫 Strawberries
♡ 👍 🚫 Pineapples
♡ 👍 🚫 Grapes
♡ 👍 🚫 Peaches

Bible Foods

♡ 👍 🚫 Fish
♡ 👍 🚫 Bread
♡ 👍 🚫 Locusts
♡ 👍 🚫 Honey
♡ 👍 🚫 Figs
♡ 👍 🚫 Grapes
♡ 👍 🚫 Olives

Wherever
YOU ARE

I'm Moses. While the Israelites and I were wandering in the wilderness, we didn't always know where we were going. But we could always see God at work all around us, no matter where we were.

God's a pretty amazing friend. He always gives you what you need, no matter where you are. You could live in the middle of a busy city or out on a farm in the country, and God will be there, showing you his love.

"The Lord is watching everywhere, keeping his eye on both the evil and the good." (Proverbs 15:3)

Draw a map of the place you live—your neighborhood, your family's farm, your city block—wherever you live. Draw the buildings, streets, paths, trees, water, and anything else you would find in the area you call home.

GOD Shows Me Where to GO

My life was full of things that weren't normal. I started out as the baby of a poor slave woman but grew up in the king's palace. I've seen a bush on fire that didn't get burned up. I've seen the land covered in frogs as far as my eyes could see. I've walked right through the middle of a sea without getting a drop of water on me.

Yep, I've seen a lot of weird stuff. Sometimes life got scary. Sometimes I didn't understand what was happening around me. But the one thing I could always count on was God guiding my steps. Through everything, God was my constant friend and showed me the way to go.

Hear Moses tell his story on page 75 in the *Friends With God Story Bible*. (Exodus 20:1–21)

When have you felt lost? How did you find your way again?

What's one way you can tell that God is watching out for you?

What are some things God has provided for you?

Three Epic Epiphanies

1. God guides your steps.

2. Since God is your friend, God will always walk every path with you.

3. "So be strong and courageous! Do not be afraid and do not panic before them. For the Lord your God will personally go ahead of you. He will neither fail you nor abandon you" (Deuteronomy 31:6).

My Top Fives

For 40 years the Israelites and I lived in the wilderness between Egypt and the Promised Land. We spent our time outside in the rocky desert, with not much to do day after day. It was kind of like being stranded on a deserted island.

What would you like to do with your time if you were stranded in the wilderness for a long, long time? List your top fives on these pages.

Top Five Songs I'd Want to Listen To

Top Five Books I'd Want to Read

Top Five Movies I'd Like to Watch

Top Five Games I'd Want to Play

The Greatest STORIES Ever Told

> Stories help us understand more about God. They give us hints about what it's like to be God's friend. My stories help you see that nothing is more powerful than God.

"Jesus always used stories and illustrations like these when speaking to the crowds. In fact, he never spoke to them without using such parables."
(Matthew 13:34)

PIP QUIZ!

What can you learn about God from your favorite movie?
What's a song that reminds you of God?

You can also learn from stories—and the people who tell them—that aren't in the Bible. List your favorites in the spaces below.

Favorite funny movie:

Favorite scary movie:

Favorite sci-fi movie:

Favorite cartoon movie:

Favorite superhero movie:

Favorite happy song:

Favorite sad song:

Favorite dance song:

Favorite video game:

Favorite funny book:

Favorite serious book:

Favorite nonfiction book:

My Life in P.I.E.
(Personal Identity Enhancement)

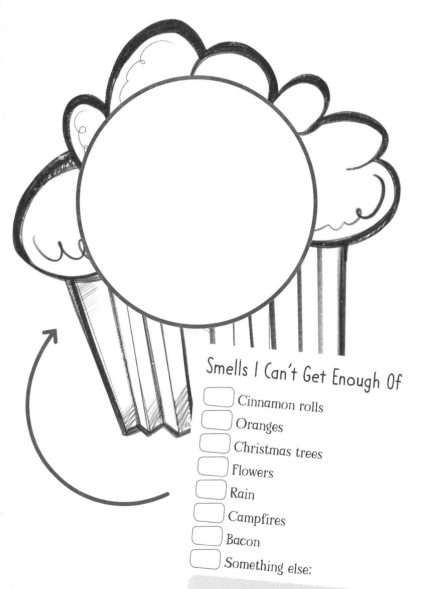

Smells I Can't Get Enough Of

- ☐ Cinnamon rolls
- ☐ Oranges
- ☐ Christmas trees
- ☐ Flowers
- ☐ Rain
- ☐ Campfires
- ☐ Bacon
- ☐ Something else:

Things I Need to Clean

Chart the dirtiest stuff you own.

- [ ] My bedroom
- [ ] My bathroom
- [ ] My hands
- [ ] My underwear
- [ ] My dog
- [ ] My hamster cage
- [ ] Something else:

Be Comfortable Versus Look Good

- [ ] Be comfortable
- [ ] Look good

Personal PRAYERS

My name is Hannah, and my biggest story started with a prayer. I wanted a baby so much that I prayed that God would give me a son. And God answered my prayer! My boy, Samuel, grew up to be a true man of God.

"I urge you, first of all, to pray for all people. Ask God to help them; intercede on their behalf, and give thanks for them." (1 Timothy 2:1)

There are lots of things you can pray for. Write some prayers on this page for yourself and the important people in your life.

Prayer asking God to teach me something:

Prayer for my mom, dad, or other important grown-up in my life:

Prayer for my brother or sister:

Prayer for my whole family:

What does it say about God as our friend
that he wants us to talk to him all the time?

♡ Love It!

👍 Like It.

🚫 Loathe It...

What can't you get enough of? What is just okay?
What do you never want to see again?
Circle your answers below.

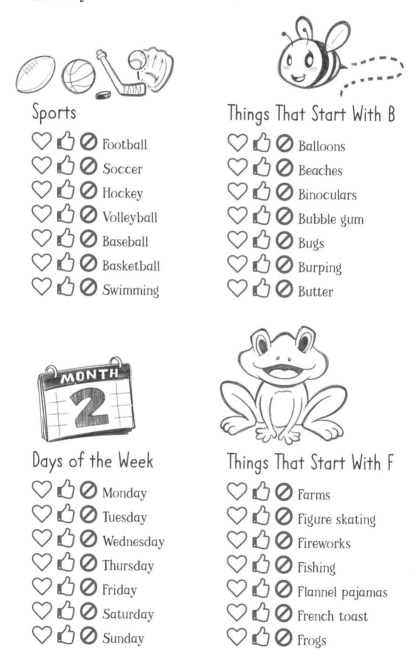

Sports
♡ 👍 🚫 Football
♡ 👍 🚫 Soccer
♡ 👍 🚫 Hockey
♡ 👍 🚫 Volleyball
♡ 👍 🚫 Baseball
♡ 👍 🚫 Basketball
♡ 👍 🚫 Swimming

Things That Start With B
♡ 👍 🚫 Balloons
♡ 👍 🚫 Beaches
♡ 👍 🚫 Binoculars
♡ 👍 🚫 Bubble gum
♡ 👍 🚫 Bugs
♡ 👍 🚫 Burping
♡ 👍 🚫 Butter

Days of the Week
♡ 👍 🚫 Monday
♡ 👍 🚫 Tuesday
♡ 👍 🚫 Wednesday
♡ 👍 🚫 Thursday
♡ 👍 🚫 Friday
♡ 👍 🚫 Saturday
♡ 👍 🚫 Sunday

Things That Start With F
♡ 👍 🚫 Farms
♡ 👍 🚫 Figure skating
♡ 👍 🚫 Fireworks
♡ 👍 🚫 Fishing
♡ 👍 🚫 Flannel pajamas
♡ 👍 🚫 French toast
♡ 👍 🚫 Frogs

My Top Fives

Top Five Cereals

Top Five Things to Put in My Lunchbox

Wonderfully MADE

The deepest and truest things about how God, my friend, created me.

The thing I'm proudest of:

The coolest thing I've ever done:

The thing I like the most about myself:

The time of day I'm happiest:

The dumbest mistake I've made:

The thing that worries me the most:

The smallest thing I'm afraid of:

The scariest thing I've ever seen:

The thing about me I'd most like to change:

The kindest thing I've done:

The most confusing thing I don't understand:

"The Lord keeps watch over you as you come and go, both now and forever." (Psalm 121:8)

Let's GO!

My name is Joshua, and I've traveled to a *lot* of places—all around the wilderness (more times than I can count), and up and down the Promised Land. It was great to see so many different sights. But the best thing about my journeys is that God was *always* with me.

Which parts of God's great world would you like to see? Write your favorite places you've *already been* in **green**, and write the places you'd like to see *someday* in **red**.

Vacation spot:

Place to people-watch:

U.S. state:

Place to go without my parents:

Place to relax:

Place to go with my best friend:

Place to read:

Fictional world:

Place to hide:

Cold place:

Hot place:

PIP QUIZ!

Why is it good to remember that God is with you wherever you go? (Read Joshua 1:9 for a clue.)

Passion PRAYERS

My name is Abigail. Talking to God is a huge part of being friends with God. God loves to hear us pray, and we can talk to God about anything, anytime, anywhere.

"And so I tell you, keep on asking, and you will receive what you ask for. Keep on seeking, and you will find. Keep on knocking, and the door will be opened to you."

(Luke 11:9)

It's good to pray for all parts of your life. Write some prayers on this page for things that are important to you.

Prayer for my school:

Prayer for my neighborhood:

Prayer for someone I know who's sick:

Prayer for my church:

My Life in P.I.E.
(Personal Identity Enhancement)

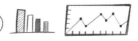

"But anyone who does not love does not know God, for God is love."

(1 John 4:8)

Fill out these P.I.E. charts to show what makes you, you.

Things I Wonder About God

Chart the questions you wonder the most about God.

- ☐ Why did God create the world?
- ☐ Why did God create me?
- ☐ What does God look like?
- ☐ Who does God hang out with in heaven?
- ☐ Does God laugh?
- ☐ Does God cry?
- ☐ Something else?

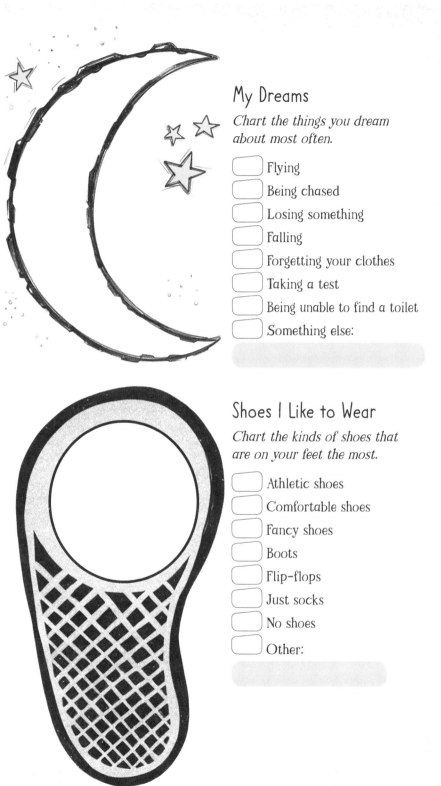

My Dreams

Chart the things you dream about most often.

- [ ] Flying
- [ ] Being chased
- [ ] Losing something
- [ ] Falling
- [ ] Forgetting your clothes
- [ ] Taking a test
- [ ] Being unable to find a toilet
- [ ] Something else:

Shoes I Like to Wear

Chart the kinds of shoes that are on your feet the most.

- [ ] Athletic shoes
- [ ] Comfortable shoes
- [ ] Fancy shoes
- [ ] Boots
- [ ] Flip-flops
- [ ] Just socks
- [ ] No shoes
- [ ] Other:

You Are ENOUGH

I'm Gideon. There was a time my people were being tormented by an army of bullies. They stole our animals, ruined our food, and made our lives miserable! But then God said he wanted *me* to take care of them.

Me? I had every reason to think I wasn't the right guy for the job. I was young, I wasn't much of a soldier, and I was afraid.

I asked God three times, "Are you *sure* you want me?" And every time, God made it clear that I was his guy. God told me I was enough. And he was right! We defeated those bullies because I followed God's instructions.

Being friends with God means *being* God's friend. In other words, it means *doing* what God asks us to do, even when we're not sure of ourselves.

Hear Gideon tell his story on page 117 in the *Friends With God Story Bible*.

(Judges 6–7)

What's one thing you're really good at? Draw a picture of yourself doing it.

What's one thing you're really bad at? Draw a picture of yourself doing it.

Write about one thing you'd like to learn to do better.

Three Epic Epiphanies

1. God believes in you. He's for you, not against you.

2. God knows that you're capable of doing more than you realize.

3. "What shall we say about such wonderful things as these? If God is for us, who can ever be against us?" (Romans 8:31).

All Kinds of
FRIENDS

Our names are Ruth and Naomi. We're best friends! We've been through a lot together, and there's nothing that can pull us apart. Friends are the most important thing you can have in life, especially the best friend of all: God!

You can read Ruth and Naomi's story of friendship on page 123 of the *Friends With God Story Bible*. (Ruth 1–2)

Who are your closest friends?
List 12 people you know;
then mark how close each
friend is to you

We kinda know each other

I could tell you a few things about them

We hang out sometimes

We're pretty close

Closest friend ever!

"Two people are better off than one, for
they can help each other succeed. If one
person falls, the other can reach out and help."
(Ecclesiastes 4:9-10)

Just One WORD

What's your home like? Did you know God lives there, too? Next to each item write one word that describes the things in your home.

My bedroom:

Kitchen:

Yard:

Living room:

Plants:

Garage:

The view:

The neighborhood:

The walls:

The smell:

My HOME

Draw a picture of your home here.

"Unless the Lord builds a house,
the work of the builders is wasted."

(Psalm 127:1)

What's Most IMPORTANT in My Life

The most important things in my life are loving God and showing love to my friend, Naomi. They're the center of my world.

God's like that with you, too. And what's important to God, your friend, should be important to you, too.

 QUIZ!

How do you know if what's important to you is also important to God? (If you want some clues about what's most important to God, read Micah 6:8 and Matthew 22:36-40.)

Fill out this scatter chart with the things that are most important to you. If it's more important to you, write the number closer to the center. If it's less important, write the number farther out.

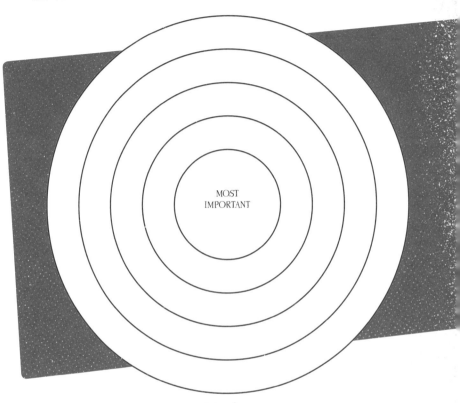

MOST
IMPORTANT

1. Spending time with friends
2. Spending time with my family
3. Having fun
4. Trying new things
5. Helping others
6. Getting smarter
7. Making art
8. Growing closer to God
9. Making money
10. Looking good
11. Something else:

Love It!
Like It.
Loathe It...

Hi! I'm David. Like you, I have lots of likes and dislikes. For example, I love God and all my brothers. I like sheep and harps. But I can't stand giants!

What about you? What can't you get enough of? What is just okay? What do you never want to see again? Circle your answers below.

Things That Start With H

♡ 👍 🚫 Hamsters
♡ 👍 🚫 Harmonicas
♡ 👍 🚫 Hats
♡ 👍 🚫 Hermit crabs
♡ 👍 🚫 Honey
♡ 👍 🚫 Hopscotch
♡ 👍 🚫 Hot dogs

Things That Start With M

♡ 👍 🚫 Magnets
♡ 👍 🚫 Marbles
♡ 👍 🚫 Marshmallows
♡ 👍 🚫 Mazes
♡ 👍 🚫 Minecraft
♡ 👍 🚫 Money
♡ 👍 🚫 Mud

Things That Start With J

♡ 👍 🚫 Jacks
♡ 👍 🚫 Jalapeños
♡ 👍 🚫 Jazz
♡ 👍 🚫 Jelly beans
♡ 👍 🚫 Jelly doughnuts
♡ 👍 🚫 Jellyfish
♡ 👍 🚫 Jewelry

Things That Start With P

♡ 👍 🚫 Paper airplanes
♡ 👍 🚫 Parties
♡ 👍 🚫 Penguins
♡ 👍 🚫 Pillow fights
♡ 👍 🚫 Piñatas
♡ 👍 🚫 Popcorn
♡ 👍 🚫 Puppets

Power PRAYERS

Prayer has always been a big part of my life. I ask God to help me through hard times, just as I would ask a great friend. I tell God how things are going in my life. And I thank God for all the wonderful things he does for me.

"The Lord hears his people when they call to him for help. He rescues them from all their troubles." (David, Psalm 34:17)

When you pray, God hears you, and God can make anything happen. Write some prayers on this page for yourself and the important people in your life.

Prayer for God to give something special to someone I know:

Prayer for someone I want to be safe:

Prayer for someone I want to be happy:

Prayer for a situation I can't control:

My Friends in P.I.E.
(Personal Identity Enhancement)

Things That Make a Good Friend

These are some qualities that make a good friend. Chart the things you like most about your human friends:

- [ ] Trust
- [ ] Laughter
- [ ] Having things in common
- [ ] Listening
- [ ] Honesty
- [ ] Encouragement
- [ ] Accepting each other
- [ ] Other:

Now chart the things you like most about your friend God:

- [ ] Trust
- [ ] Laughter
- [ ] Having things in common
- [ ] Listening
- [ ] Honesty
- [ ] Encouragement
- [ ] Accepting each other
- [ ] Other:

"Fix your thoughts on what is true, and honorable, and right, and pure, and lovely, and admirable. Think about things that are excellent and worthy of praise." (Philippians 4:8)

Things I Like to Do With My Friends

These are some things you do with your friends. Chart the things you do most with your human friends:

- Play together
- Talk with each other
- Watch videos together
- Draw or make art together
- Eat together
- Something else:

Now chart the things you do most with your friend God:

- Play together
- Talk with each other
- Watch videos together
- Draw or make art together
- Eat together
- Something else:

Wonderfully
MADE

The wonderful truths about how God gives me joy:

Things That Make Me Smile

The oldest thing I own:

The ugliest thing I own but love anyway:

The thing I'm most careful with:

The thing that makes me calmest:

The most breakable thing I own:

The largest thing I own:

The smallest thing I own:

The softest thing I own:

The smelliest thing in my house:

My biggest collection:

PIP QUIZ!

God loves to give gifts to his friends. What's the most valuable thing God has ever given you? (If you need some examples, read 1 Corinthians 12:7-11.)

My Top Fives

Top Five Sports Teams

Top Five Games to Play With Friends

 **PIP** QUIZ!

What do you think God cares about when it comes to sports?
(If you want some ideas, look for clues in Galatians 5:22-23.)

How I FLOW

What I Do on Road Trips

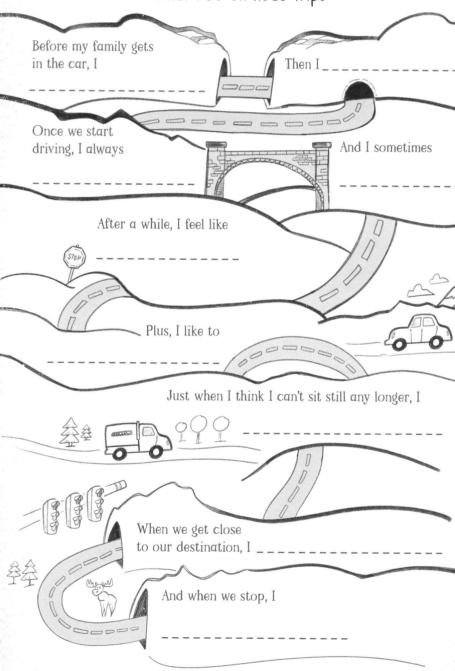

Before my family gets
in the car, I

_ _ _ _ _ _ _ _ _ _ _ _ _ _ _

Then I _ _ _ _ _ _ _ _ _ _ _ _ _ _

Once we start
driving, I always

_ _ _ _ _ _ _ _ _ _ _ _ _ _ _

And I sometimes

_ _ _ _ _ _ _ _ _ _ _

After a while, I feel like

_ _ _ _ _ _ _ _ _ _ _ _ _ _ _

Plus, I like to

_ _ _ _ _ _ _ _ _ _ _ _ _ _ _

Just when I think I can't sit still any longer, I

_ _ _ _ _ _ _ _ _ _ _ _ _

When we get close
to our destination, I _ _ _ _ _ _ _ _ _ _ _ _ _ _ _ _

And when we stop, I

_ _ _ _ _ _ _ _ _ _ _ _ _ _

The Weather and Me

Whenever it's sunny, I like to

I always

when it's really hot outside.

But when the clouds roll in, I

If it's raining, I usually

Thunder and lightning make me

When the wind kicks up, I

Snow is the one thing that always makes me

And when the air turns super cold, I feel like

"And I am convinced that nothing can ever separate us from God's love. Neither death nor life, neither angels nor demons, neither our fears for today nor our worries about tomorrow—not even the powers of hell can separate us from God's love. No power in the sky above or in the earth below—indeed, nothing in all creation will ever be able to separate us from the love of God that is revealed in Christ Jesus our Lord." (Romans 8:38-39)

Perfect PRAYERS

It's me, David, again. I love to pray. I wrote lots and lots and *lots* of poems called psalms. Psalms are my prayers to God, my best friend. They're the perfect way to let God know how I'm feeling.

On the next page, write your own psalms that thank God for the things in your life. Here is an example of a psalm in the Bible:

"I lay down and slept, yet I woke up in safety, for the Lord was watching over me. I am not afraid of ten thousand enemies who surround me on every side" (Psalm 3:5-6).

"This is the day the Lord has made. We will rejoice and be glad in it." (Psalm 118:24)

You can also read David's Psalm 23 in
the *Friends With God Story Bible*.

Psalm for something you're thankful for in your bedroom:

Psalm thanking God for something you love about your family:

Psalm thanking God for the good people in your life:

Psalm telling God the reasons you love him so much:

My Life in P.I.E.
(Personal Identity Enhancement)

Things I'm Afraid Of

Chart the things that scare you the most:

- [ ] The dark
- [ ] Spiders
- [ ] Being alone
- [ ] Animals that bite
- [ ] Bullies
- [ ] Something else:

- [ ] High places
- [ ] Snakes
- [ ] Water
- [ ] Lightning
- [ ] Clowns

"And don't forget to do good and to share with those in need. These are the sacrifices that please God."
(Hebrews 13:16)

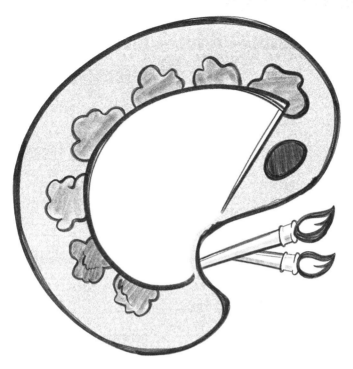

Ways I'm Creative

Chart the ways you're most creative:

- [ ] Painting/drawing
- [ ] Cooking
- [ ] Making
- [ ] Fashion
- [ ] Something else:

- [ ] Writing
- [ ] Dancing
- [ ] Tinkering
- [ ] Pretending

PIP QUIZ!

What are three ways God helps you?
(For one hint, read Psalm 56:3-4.)

God Makes Me STRONG

I am Queen Esther. I may be a queen, but I'm actually a pretty normal person. I love my family, I enjoy hanging out with my friends, and I get scared when bad things happen.

When things got dangerous for my people and me, I did what any normal person can do: I trusted in God. God put me in the right place at the right time, and he gave me the strength to be brave.

God does that for you, too. God can make you strong when you need him to. When it comes time to stand up and do the right thing, God knows you can do it.

Hear Esther tell her story on page 185 in the *Friends With God Story Bible*. (Esther 5:1–8; 8:1–17)

What's something that surprises you about Esther's story?

What do you think it would be like to be a queen or king?

What's one way God has made you strong?

Three Epic Epiphanies

1. God is stronger than anything.

2. Since God is your friend, God will make you strong at the right time.

3. "For I can do everything through Christ, who gives me strength" (Philippians 4:13).

A Royal
FRIEND

When you're friends with God, you're friends with royalty!
After all, God is the King of kings. *You* are a friend of the King!

Think about the different things God does for you as your friend.
God is your protector, your creator, your comforter, and your
teacher. Isn't it wonderful to have a friend who is all those things?

On these pages, design four crowns that show how God is your
protector, your creator, your comforter, and your teacher.
Be creative and have fun!

Protector

Creator

"O Lord of Heaven's Armies, God of Israel, you are enthroned between the mighty cherubim! You alone are God of all the kingdoms of the earth. You alone created the heavens and the earth." (Isaiah 37:16)

Comforter

Teacher

My Top Fives

Top Five Things About Being a Kid

Top Five Ways to Show People You Love Them

PIP QUIZ!

The Bible says in 1 John 4:20-21 that when we love others, we're loving God, too. After all, they're God's friends, too, and all friends love each other. Who's one person you can show God's love to?

Top Five Places to Have Fun

Top Five Games to Play With My Friends

 QUIZ!

God loves for us to be joyful. What's one way you can have fun with God?

Three Little WORDS

"Whenever we have the chance, we should do good to everyone."

(Galatians 6:10)

God was such a great friend to me that he put courageous people in my life—like my cousin Mordecai—to help me be brave. Since God is your friend, he's put amazing people in your life, too.

In the spaces below, write their names; then write three words that best describe them.

Favorite friend:

Favorite teacher:

Favorite funny person:

Favorite smart person:

Favorite kind person:

Favorite strong person:

Favorite talkative person:

Favorite quiet person:

Favorite athlete:

Favorite Bible character:

What do you think are three of God's favorite qualities for friends?
(For some ideas, read Galatians 5:22-23.)

What do you think God would say are his three favorite things about you?

What's on Your MIND?

What do you think about most of the time? Fill the brain with pictures of things you think about most often.

Bonus: How can you show that all those things you're thinking about are connected to God? (Read Matthew 6:33 to see what the Bible has to say about it.)

"And now, dear brothers and sisters, one final thing. Fix your thoughts on what is true, and honorable, and right, and pure, and lovely, and admirable. Think about things that are excellent and worthy of praise."
(Philippians 4:8)

My Brain

Wonderfully MADE

God made me a very beautiful woman, which was the reason I became a queen. God made all of us different, and God doesn't make mistakes. God made you just the way he wanted you, and God thinks *you* are beautiful!

"We are God's masterpiece."
(Ephesians 2:10)

About Me...

There are lots of wonderful things about you. Write about them below.

Favorite scar:

Favorite thing to do at night:

Favorite thing to draw
with sidewalk chalk:

Favorite weird fact about me:

Favorite thing about rainy days:

Favorite thing I'd like
to do but never get to:

Favorite thing I'm most proud of:

Favorite thing my family does
together:

Favorite way I like to help others:

Favorite thing I see when
I look in the mirror:

About God...

Favorite thing about the Bible:

Favorite reason to love God:

Favorite thing to talk about with God:

Whatcha THINK?

My name is Daniel, and I was put in a room full of hungry lions! Thankfully, my friend God was with me the whole time and kept me safe.

I hope *you* never get stuck in a lion's cage! Are there some hard things you would try to do some day? Fill in the faces to show what you think about the stuff below.

You Want Me to Do What?

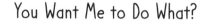

☹ 😐 ☺ Skydive

☹ 😐 ☺ Swim with sharks

☹ 😐 ☺ Ride the world's fastest roller coaster

☹ 😐 ☺ Climb a tall mountain

☹ 😐 ☺ Drive a race car

☹ 😐 ☺ Run through fire

☹ 😐 ☺ Wrestle an alligator

☹ 😐 ☺ Run a marathon

☹ 😐 ☺ Ski an Olympic ski jump

☹ 😐 ☺ Eat a grasshopper

☹ = I'll never do that!

😐 = I might try that.

☺ = I can do that!

Read Daniel's story on page 213 in the *Friends With God Story Bible*. (Daniel 6)

You Want Me to Draw What?

Draw a picture of yourself doing something extraordinary.

How would God help you do this amazing thing?

How Can I "SEE" God?

How can you be friends with someone you can't see or hear? After all, we can't *see* God. And yet...we can.

We see God in the good things other Christians do. (See Matthew 5:14-16.) Name one Christian friend you've seen do something good:

We see God whenever we witness love, joy, peace, patience, kindness, goodness, faithfulness, gentleness, and self-control—the fruits of the Spirit. (See Galatians 5:22-23.) Name one relative you've seen show one of the fruits of the Spirit:

We see God in the hungry, the thirsty, the strangers, those needing clothes, the sick, and those in prison. (See Matthew 25:31-46.) Name someone you know who helps take care of someone in need:

"I love all who love me. Those who search will surely find me." (Proverbs 8:17)

We see God in nature and throughout all the beauty
and intricacies of his creation. (See Romans 1:19-20.)
Name a place in nature that reminds you of God:

We see God through the life of Jesus. "Christ is the visible image
of the invisible God" (Colossians 1:15). Name your favorite story
about Jesus:

We see God in all the things he gives us, like food and clothes.
(See Philippians 4:19 and Matthew 6:31-33.) Name one thing
you own that you're thankful for:

We see God in all the good things that come into our lives.
(See James 1:17.) Name one good thing that's happened in your life:

My SCHOOL

My name is Josiah, and when I was just 8 years old, I became king of my nation. I had a lot to learn, and I spent most of my time discovering as much as I could about God and all his books. Friends like to learn as much about each other as they can.

You're learning things, too. What's your school like? Write one word next to each item that best describes the things at your school.

Cafeteria food:

Playground:

Gym:

My teacher:

Chairs and desks:

Bathrooms:

Bus driver:

Friends:

Principal:

Library:

Homework:

My Top Fives

Top Five Things About School

Top Five Ways to Remember God at School

"For the Lord grants wisdom!
From his mouth come knowledge
and understanding." (Proverbs 2:6)

Wise Up

My name is Solomon. When God told me I could have anything I wanted, I knew exactly what I would ask for. I told God I wanted wisdom. I knew wisdom would enable me to make smart decisions and know how to do the right thing.

Wisdom helps me see the world the way God sees it. Just think: God is my best friend, and God is wiser than anyone!

Since God is your friend, he's ready to give you wisdom, too. All you have to do is ask for it.

Wisdom may not give you a palace, golden treasures, or a mighty army. But God's wisdom can help you be smarter and kinder in your everyday life. The wiser you can be as a kid, the wiser you can be when you grow up.

Hear Solomon tell his story on page 151 in the *Friends With God Story Bible*. (1 Kings 3; Proverbs 1:1–7; 2:1–22)

Wisdom is another way to know God is by your side. What's one wise thing God has helped you do right?

Why do you think some people don't try to be wise?

What's one thing you can do to get a little wiser today?

Three Epic Epiphanies

1. God is wise.

2. Since God is your friend, God will give you wisdom when you ask for it.

3. "Doing wrong is fun for a fool, but living wisely brings pleasure to the sensible" (Proverbs 10:23).

TIME Will Tell

"For everything there is a season, a time for every activity under heaven." (Ecclesiastes 3:1)

About Me...

Favorite day of the year:

Favorite time of day:

Favorite holiday:

Favorite thing about autumn:

Favorite thing about summer:

Favorite thing about winter:

Favorite thing about spring:

Favorite thing about Christmas:

Favorite thing to do on a weekend:

Favorite thing to do on a Monday:

Favorite time period I'd like to travel to:

About God...

What do you think God spends his time doing?
(Look for some clues in Psalm 121.)

How much time do you think God wants to spend with you?
(Think about what 1 Thessalonians 5:17 says.)

What do you think is God's favorite holiday? Jesus' birthday?
Passover? The day Jesus rose from the dead? Why do you think that?

Are there times you feel closer to God than others? When?

God's Great
CREATION

I know a thing or two about the biggest and best. God gave me the biggest and best riches, as well as the most beautiful kingdom in the world. But the most important thing he gave me was wisdom. And God gave me wisdom simply because I asked for it.

PIP QUIZ!

Sometimes friends surprise us. Where do you think God is most likely to show up in your life?

What do you love most about the amazing world God created?

The wettest place I've ever been: _____

The driest place I've ever been: _____

_____ is the most crowded place I've ever been.

_____ is the biggest building I've ever been in.

The smallest room I've ever been in: _____

The tallest building I've ever been in: _____

_____ is the coolest place I've ever been.

Most boring place I've ever been: _____

Draw a picture of what you think is the most beautiful place on earth.

Go With the FLOW

Being a king keeps me busy from the time I wake up until the moment I fall asleep again. But I always make time to focus on God, too. No matter what I'm doing, I take time to pray every morning, day, and night.

How do you spend your time? Fill in these charts to show what you do every morning and night.

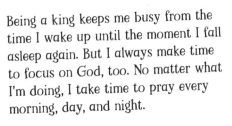

My Morning Routine

When I wake up I

Next, I

After that, I

Then I

I usually

And I always

Finally, I

My Bedtime Routine

When I start to feel sleepy, I

As I start to get ready for bed, I

Then I usually

After that, I

Next, I

I never forget to

When I'm finally in bed, I

before I fall asleep.

PIP QUIZ!

How do you include God in your day?

My Life in P.I.E.
(Personal Identity Enhancement)

Things I'd Like to Change About Myself

Chart the things you think might be better if they were different:

- [ ] My physical appearance
- [ ] Where I live
- [ ] My friends
- [ ] My clothes
- [ ] My smarts
- [ ] My emotions
- [ ] Nothing
- [ ] Something else:

"Thank you for making me so wonderfully complex! Your workmanship is marvelous—how well I know it." (Psalm 139:14)

How I Like My Peanut Butter and Jelly

Chart how much of each would make a perfect sandwich:

☐ Peanut butter
☐ Jelly

Words I Use the Most

Chart how often you use these words:

☐ Awesome   ☐ Cool   ☐ Dude

☐ What?   ☐ Huh   ☐ OMG

☐ Stuff   ☐ Uh   ☐ Yo

☐ Something else: _____

Words to the WISE

Thanks to God, I was one of the wisest people who ever lived. But the wisest thing I did was learning to be a friend of God.

I shared a lot of my wisdom in the book of Proverbs. A proverb is a wise saying. Use the words below (and a few of your own, if you want) to write your very own proverbs. Pray first and ask God to help you.

Wise Words

you	give	heart	listen
God	fill	all	quiet
pray	want	peace	more
wait	always	life	go
see	care	touch	good
great	very	love	kind
still	with	look	feel
friend	and	make	wise

"If you need wisdom, ask our generous God, and he will give it to you."

(James 1:5)

My Proverbs

How can wisdom help your friendships with God and other people?
(There are great Scripture clues in Proverbs 27:17 and Proverbs 12:15.)

The opposite of what makes me happy is:

 The opposite of what makes me mad is:

The opposite of following God is:

 The opposite of giving a gift is:

The opposite of praying is:

 The opposite of helping my mom is:

The opposite of being creative is:

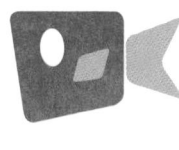 The opposite of breaking something is:

The opposite of fighting with someone is:

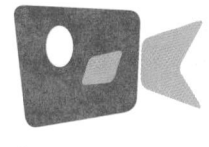

 The opposite of following instructions is:

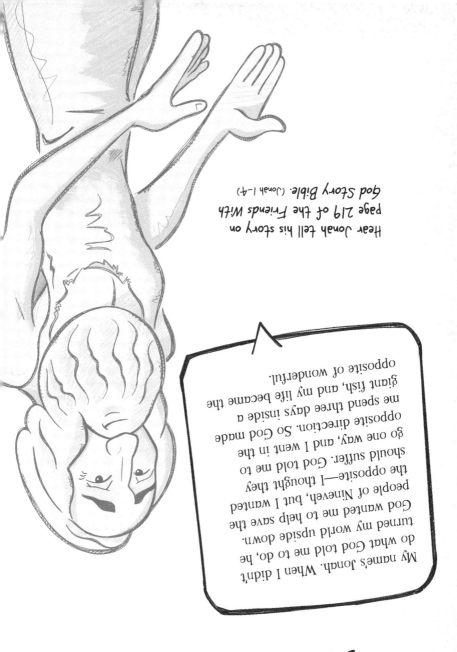

My name's Jonah. When I didn't do what God told me to do, he turned my world upside down. God wanted me to help save the people of Nineveh, but I wanted the opposite—I thought they should suffer. God told me to go one way, and I went in the opposite direction. So God made me spend three days inside a giant fish, and my life became the opposite of wonderful.

Hear Jonah tell his story on page 219 of the Friends With God Story Bible. (Jonah 1–4)

Turning My World
UPSIDE DOWN

Once Upon a TIME

Whenever you see a whale, you might be reminded of my story. People love telling my story because it helps them understand what it means to be friends with God.

"Come and listen, all you who fear God, and I will tell you what he did for me." (Psalm 66:16)

Everyone has a story, including you!
Fill in the blanks on this page to tell *your* story.
Tell a story about what you hope might happen in your future.

Once upon a time, there was a kid named _____ (your name)

This kid loved _____ and _____.

Every day, _____ (your name) did the same old thing,

which was _____. But _____ (your name)

really wanted to _____. Then one day, something changed.

Instead of doing the same old thing, _____ (your name) tried

this instead: _____. It was different, and even

a little scary, but it was also exciting! It made _____ (your name)

feel _____. The next day _____ (he/she) did it again. Soon,

_____ (your name) became really good at _____.

But there was still one big problem, which was _____.

But _____ (your name) didn't give up. Because God was

_____ (his/her) best friend, _____ (your name) knew _____ (he/she)

could overcome the problem. So the very next day,

_____ (your name) tried _____.

It worked! People loved it! It made _____ (your name)

feel very _____. So now _____ (he/she) doesn't do the same

old thing anymore. _____ (your name) spends all _____ (his/her)

extra time doing what _____ (he/she) loves most: _____.

Talk to GOD

"So now we can rejoice in our wonderful new relationship with God because our Lord Jesus Christ has made us friends of God."
(Romans 5:11)

I'm Mary. God gave me a very special job, and that was to be Jesus' mom. Being a mother can be hard sometimes, but it's also my most favorite thing in the world. I love Jesus so much! And I know you love Jesus, too.

(And he loves you back!)

What do you love most about Jesus? Take a minute to tell God.

- Tell God what you think about Jesus.

- Thank God for sending Jesus to make it possible for us to be friends with God.

Write down what you prayed right here:

Read Mary's story on page 231 of the *Friends With God Story Bible*. (Matthew 2:13–23)

STOP — AND — GO

Stop what you're doing and *go* do something for God! Christmas is the time of year people celebrate when God came to earth as a person to let us know he understands us. That's called empathy—seeing the world through someone else's eyes—and it's a great quality for friends to have.

Make a small Christmas garland bracelet for a person you care about. It's easy! Follow the rectangle pattern here on this page to cut out about 15 rectangles from red and green construction paper or Christmas wrapping.

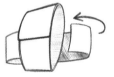

Take one rectangle and glue it into a small circle. Then take the next rectangle and loop it through the first circle, gluing the ends together. Add the rest of the rectangles until you have a complete bracelet. Then give the bracelet to your friend and tell that person that Jesus loves him or her.

••••••> trace outline ••••••••

Write the name of the person you gave the bracelet to, and then describe what happened.

A Friend INDEED

We're best friends! God brought us together and showed us some very special things. Having great friends makes life so much better.

What about your friends? Write about all the wonderful friends you have. Write their names, followed by one word that describes them best.

My Friends

Most faithful:

Kindest:

Happiest:

Fanciest:

Funniest:

Most dramatic:

Most mysterious:

Friendliest:

"Those who love money will never have enough. How meaningless to think that wealth brings true happiness!" (Ecclesiastes 5:10)

My Top Fives

Top Five Things to Buy for $1

Top Five Things to Buy for $1 Million

PIP QUIZ!

What's one way you can honor God with your money?
(Find one possible answer by reading Matthew 19:21.)

Love One ANOTHER

My name is Jesus. God sent me to the world to show people what *love* is all about. Love is the greatest thing ever! God loves you *so much*. And you know what makes God happiest? When we love him back and love other people.

I talk about love all the time. Whenever people have a problem, I show them how love can make their problems better. Whenever people ask me what they should do with their lives, I tell them to love God and others. And whenever people do bad things to me, God helps me love them anyway.

Love can be the best thing in your life, too. When you love the people around you, it makes you feel better. It makes them feel better, too. And that makes your friend God happy. *Very* happy.

There are lots of ways to show love to other people. What's your favorite way to love your friends? Draw a picture of you showing love to someone.

Hear Jesus tell his story on page 273 in the *Friends With God Story Bible*.
(Matthew 27:27–28:10)

Name three simple things you can do every day that show people you care about them.

What's one thing that can make it hard for you to show love to someone else?

Draw a picture of how you think it makes God feel when we love him and other people.

Three Epic Epiphanies

1. Jesus is God's Son, and because he loved us so much, he died and came back to life so we can be God's friends forever.

2. Jesus made it possible for us to be friends with God.

3. "For this is how God loved the world: He gave his one and only Son, so that everyone who believes in him will not perish but have eternal life. God sent his Son into the world not to judge the world, but to save the world through him" (John 3:16-17).

My Favorite MEMORIES

"We have happy memories of the godly." (Proverbs 10:7)

My life is full of amazing times when God was with me and my family. Like the time I was a kid and my family was traveling. My parents thought I had gotten lost, but I was actually back at the Temple talking to people about God.

PIP QUIZ!

What's one good way to remind yourself that God is always near? (Look up Hebrews 13:5 for one possible clue.)

I'm sure you have lots of memories.
Draw a picture of you during each of these times in your life:

The time I was happiest:

The time I was really mad:

The time I was the saddest:

The time I was really confused:

My Life in P.I.E.
(Personal Identity Enhancement)

Day Versus Night

Chart how much you prefer the different times of your day:

☐ Day
☐ Night

"But we are looking forward to the new heavens and new earth he has promised, a world filled with God's righteousness."

(2 Peter 3:13)

Hot or Cold?

Chart how much you'd rather be hot or cold:

- [ ] Hot
- [ ] Cold

How I Like the Weather

Chart which kinds of weather make you happiest:

- [ ] Sunny
- [ ] Cloudy
- [ ] Rainy
- [ ] Snowy
- [ ] Windy
- [ ] Something else:

Hot

Cold

PIP QUIZ!

What have you learned from God that you never want to forget?

EPIPHANY

We shepherds had one of the most special epiphanies of all time: We got to see Jesus right after he was born. We were some of Jesus' very first friends. Wow!

Many people celebrate a holiday called Epiphany in the first week of January, right after Christmas. It's a day to remember the time God came to earth as a human. Celebrating the birth of Jesus can be a special time of epiphany for you, too, as you look for God in your own life. It's like bringing light to the darkness.

Imagine what it would have been like if you had been one of us shepherds at the manger or one of the wise men bringing gifts to little Jesus.

"Jesus spoke to the people once more and said, 'I am the light of the world. If you follow me, you won't have to walk in darkness, because you will have the light that leads to life.'"
(John 8:12)

You can hear the shepherds tell their story on page 225 of the *Friends With God Story Bible.*
(Luke 2:1–20)

"So the Word became human and made his home among us. He was full of unfailing love and faithfulness. And we have seen his glory, the glory of the Father's one and only Son."
(John 1:14)

What do you think Jesus looked like as a baby?

What would you say to Jesus' mother, Mary?

What gift would you have given Jesus?

What prayer would you pray for baby Jesus?

God Through YOU

Since Jesus isn't walking around on the earth with us right now, he needs us to be his friends to the people around us. We are Jesus' body while he's gone, and we can use our hands, feet, eyes, ears, and mouths to show God's love to others.

Top Five Things to Do With My Hands

Top Five Things to Do With My Feet

"All of you together are Christ's body, and each of you is a part of it."
(1 Corinthians 12:27)

My Top Fives

Top Five Things to Do With My Eyes

Top Five Things to Do With My Ears

 QUIZ!

Describe one way God has helped you use your hands or feet to do something good for someone else.

God Gave Me SKILLS

We're Aquila and Priscilla. Everyone is really good at something. We're really good at making tents. Because God wants us to honor him in *everything* we do, God wants us to serve him, even while we make tents.

God made you really good at something, too, because he's the kind of friend who wants the best for you. Use this chart to show what you're good at...and not-so-good at.

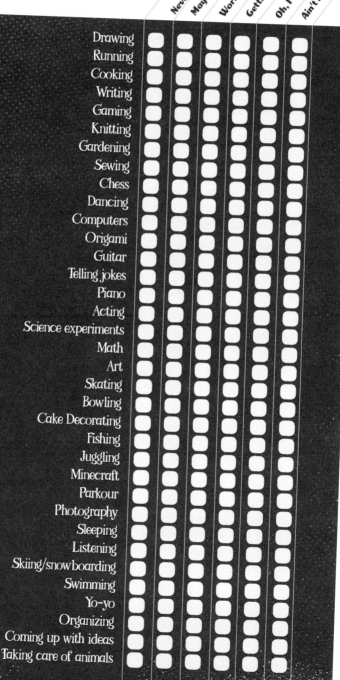

	Never	Maybe someday	Working on it	Getting better	Oh, I've got this	Ain't no one better!
Drawing						
Running						
Cooking						
Writing						
Gaming						
Knitting						
Gardening						
Sewing						
Chess						
Dancing						
Computers						
Origami						
Guitar						
Telling jokes						
Piano						
Acting						
Science experiments						
Math						
Art						
Skating						
Bowling						
Cake Decorating						
Fishing						
Juggling						
Minecraft						
Parkour						
Photography						
Sleeping						
Listening						
Skiing/snowboarding						
Swimming						
Yo-yo						
Organizing						
Coming up with ideas						
Taking care of animals						

How I LOOK

My name is John the Baptist. People thought I was a little strange because I lived out in the wilderness. I wore camel skins for my clothes, and I usually ate locusts for lunch. I took a lot of baths, though. My favorite thing to do was baptize people for God. I wanted them to change their ways so they could be friends of God, too.

Hear John the Baptist tell his story on page 237 of the Friends With God Story Bible. (John 1:19-34)

Everyone looks a little different and wears different kinds of clothes. What do you look like? Draw pictures of yourself and some of your favorite clothes.

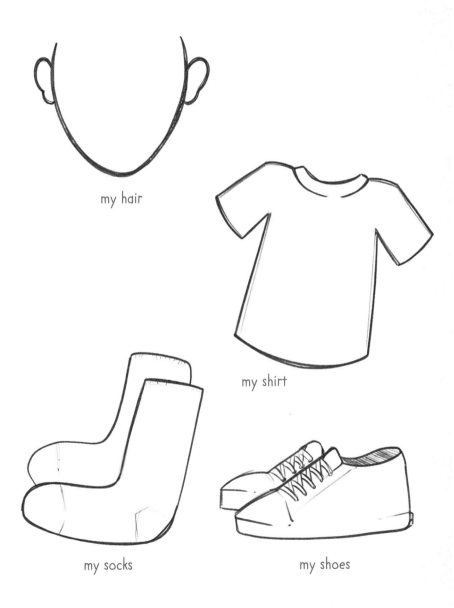

my hair

my shirt

my socks

my shoes

Talk to GOD

"For God in all his fullness was pleased to live in Christ."
(Colossians 1:19)

I had a true epiphany when I baptized Jesus. When Jesus came up out of the water, God sent a dove down from heaven, and it floated above Jesus' head. Then God said, "This is my dearly loved Son, who brings me great joy" (Matthew 3:17). Friends love and support each other.

This journal has been full of your epiphanies—ways that you see God in the world around you. Take a moment right now to talk to God about your epiphanies.

- Tell God what you've learned most about him by filling out this book.

- Tell God what you've learned most about yourself by filling out this book.

Write down what you prayed right here:

STOP
— AND —

GO

Stop what you're doing and *go* do something for God! It's always exciting to hear other friends' stories about how they've seen God working in their lives. People want to hear about your God sightings, too. You can send them an encouraging note about your epiphany on a homemade postcard.

Ask a grown-up to help you find some card stock paper; then cut it into three rectangles that are each 4 inches by 6 inches. On one side of each card, draw a picture of one way you've seen God in your life. It could be as simple as seeing God in nature or something amazing like God answering your prayer. On the other side of the postcard, write the person's address on the right half. On the left half, write a sentence or two about how you saw God in your life. Then have a grown-up help you send your postcards to three people who need to be encouraged by God.

Hi, Aunt Jane!
Today I saw a beautiful sunrise, and it reminded me that I can always count on God to show up every day in my life. He's such a dependable friend! I love you!

Place Stamp Here

List the three people you made the postcards for, and what you said to them:

1.

2.

3.

Bless This FOOD

It's me, Jesus! Food is a big part of everyone's life. Whenever we eat, it's a chance to thank God for providing food for us.

"Jesus replied, 'I am the bread of life. Whoever comes to me will never be hungry again. Whoever believes in me will never be thirsty.'" (John 6:35)

What do you like to eat? If I made you a meal from
Bible times, it would probably be some fish and bread.
Draw me a picture of a meal you would eat with me
if I came over to your house.

Because YUM!

You can find food in many stories in the Bible. People love to eat! And food brings people together. You can't stay enemies when you eat together as friends.

Fill out this scatter chart with the meals you think are the tastiest in the center, and less tasty toward the edge of the circles. Draw the symbol where you think it should go in the circle.

"Since everything God created is good, we should not reject any of it but receive it with thanks. For we know it is made acceptable by the word of God and prayer."
(I Timothy 4:4–5)

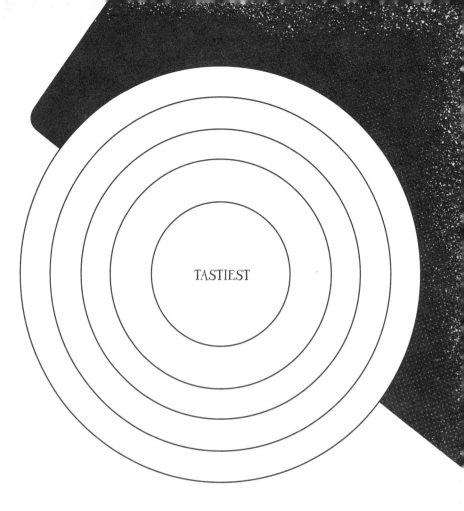

TASTIEST

 Pizza

 Tacos

 Spaghetti

 Meatloaf

 Burgers

 Pancakes

 Steak and potatoes

 Salad

 Chinese food

 Corndogs

 Fried chicken

 Mac and cheese

 Something else:

Friends With GOD

God isn't just something you study or learn about. God wants *you* to be his real friend. But how can you hang out with someone you can't see or touch?

Think about the things that make a true friendship. Below, write the names of human friends who fit each quality.

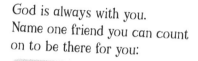

God is always with you. Name one friend you can count on to be there for you:

God always cares about you. Name one friend who really cares about you:

God is always ready to listen to you. Name one friend you like talking to:

"So now we can rejoice in our wonderful new relationship with God because our Lord Jesus Christ has made us friends of God." (Romans 5:11)

God wants the best for your life.
Name one friend who helps you be a better person:

God loves you, no matter what.
Name one friend who accepts you for who you are:

God loves spending time with you.
Name one friend you spend a lot of time with:

God gives you good things.
Name one friend who's given you a gift:

Friendship Bracelet

A lot of people make and wear friendship bracelets to show everyone how much they love a friend. What do you think a friendship bracelet with God would look like? Draw it on the wrist here.

One Big Happy FAMILY

There are many of kinds of families. Some have lots of brothers and sisters, while others have tons of cousins, aunts, and uncles. You might have a close neighbor or teacher who feels like a part of your family. Some people say their pets are part of their family, too!

God is amazingly generous! God gave you a family. Like our friends, every family member is different. They have different talents, skills, and personalities that make them unique. And God has given every one of them something that makes them special.

"Believe in the Lord Jesus and you will be saved, along with everyone in your household." (Acts 16:31)

My Family

Write the names of your family members below.

Oldest:

Youngest:

Quietest:

Loudest:

Most energetic:

Calmest:

Best cook:

Most creative:

Most patient:

Most cheerful:

Most adventurous:

Hardest working:

Best listener:

Wisest:

PIP QUIZ!

How has God shown love to you through your family?

Lots of SMILES

Top Five Emojis
Draw your five favorite emojis!

"Always be full of joy in the
Lord. I say it again—rejoice!"
(Philippians 4:4)

Top Five Jobs I Might Want to Do When I Grow Up

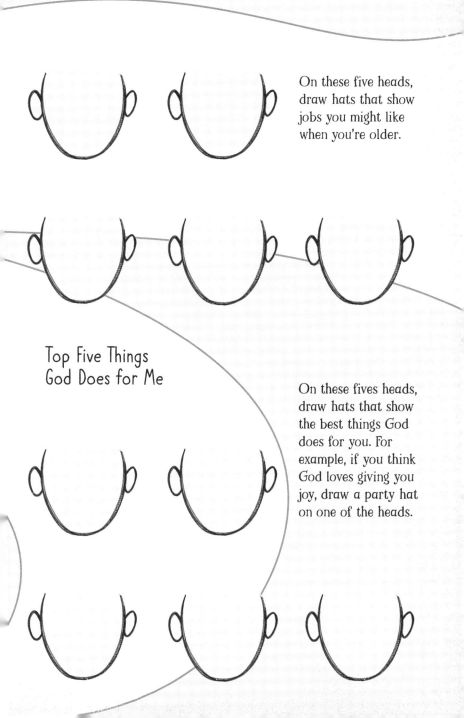

On these five heads, draw hats that show jobs you might like when you're older.

Top Five Things God Does for Me

On these fives heads, draw hats that show the best things God does for you. For example, if you think God loves giving you joy, draw a party hat on one of the heads.

You'll also love...

Friends With God Story Bible:
Why God Loves People Like Me

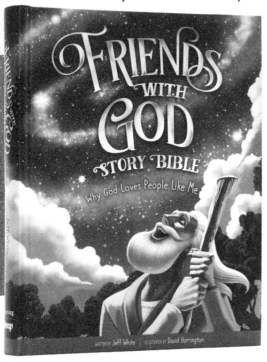

FREE Bible App

Experience the Bible in a more personal way with the free *Friends With God* app.

Friends With God
Devotions for Kids

Friends With God
Sing-Along Songs
Music CD

J eff White is a lead content developer for Group Publishing, where he's written or co-written 15 books for church ministry and faith development. He has a passion for helping people grow their creativity and leads creativity workshops at ministry conferences around the country. A graduate of Biola University, Jeff has also published several books for young readers, including *The Runaway Candy Cane*.

David Harrington's love for art began at an early age when he drew on everything, which eventually led to a career in illustration. He graduated from the Art Center College of Design in Pasadena, where he earned a bachelor's degree in fine arts with honors. David has illustrated numerous children's books and enjoys snowboarding, surfing, and spending time with his wife and children in Laguna Hills, California.